William M. Gaines's
HOWLING
MAD

ALBERT B. FELDSTEIN, Editor

A SIGNET BOOK from
NEW AMERICAN LIBRARY
TIMES MIRROR

New York and Scarborough, Ontario
The New English Library Limited, London

Published as a SIGNET BOOK by arrangement with E. C. Publications, Inc., who have authorized this softcover edition.

SIXTH PRINTING

 SIGNET TRADEMARK REG. U.S. PAT. OFF. AND FOREIGN COUNTRIES
REGISTERED TRADEMARK—MARCA REGISTRADA
HECHO EN CHICAGO, U.S.A.

SIGNET, SIGNET CLASSICS, SIGNETTE, MENTOR AND PLUME BOOKS
are published *in the United States* by
The New American Library, Inc.,
1301 Avenue of the Americas, New York, New York 10019,
in Canada by The New American Library of Canada Limited,
81 Mack Avenue, Scarborough, 704, Ontario,
in the United Kingdom by The New English Library Limited,
Barnard's Inn, Holborn, London, E.C. 1, England

FIRST PRINTING, OCTOBER, 1967

PRINTED IN THE UNITED STATES OF AMERICA

IF you are *purr*-secuted by the *purr*-veyors of *purr*-verse *purr*-suits on Television... and...

IF you are *purr*-turbed by the *purr*-functory *purr*-formances of Hollywood *purr*-sonages... and...

IF you are *purr*-meated with the *purr*-fumed *purr*-jury *purr*-petrated by Madison Avenue ...and...

IF you are *purr*-ennially *purr*-plexed by the *purr*-fidious *purr*se-packing *purr*-sona non grata in Politics...

THEN you should stop *purr*-rusing this *purr*-tinent, *purr*-poseful, and *purr*-ceptive paperback... *purr*-ambulate over to the *purr*-sonnel in charge... and *purr*-chase...

HOWLING
MAD

HOWLING MAD

Here is another MAD Primer.

It is the 431st Primer we have run.

Why do we run so many Primers?

Because Primers are easy to write.

Any idiot can write a Primer.

Even you can write a Primer.

Wouldn't you like to write a Primer for us?

Wouldn't you like to send us thousands of Primers?

Yes, yes, yes.

Soon we will have nothing but Primers in the magazine.

Soon we will not need writers.

Then we will have more money for ourselves.

Then we will become rich.

What fun it will be to become rich.

Like the people in this Primer:

THE MAD
CELEBRITY
PRIMER

MY FIRST
INTRODUCTION
TO THE
"GREATS"
OF OUR TIME

By Biff Bang (Murray Zoppelzorg), **Lance Boyle** (Seymour Fenemble),
Joy Euphoria (Zelda Greesgurgle) **and Larry Siegel** (Larry Siegel)

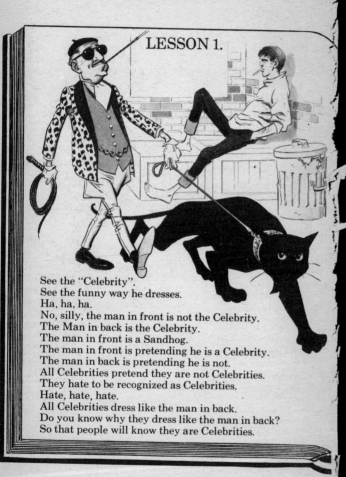

LESSON 1.

See the "Celebrity".
See the funny way he dresses.
Ha, ha, ha.
No, silly, the man in front is not the Celebrity.
The Man in back is the Celebrity.
The man in front is a Sandhog.
The man in front is pretending he is a Celebrity.
The man in back is pretending he is not.
All Celebrities pretend they are not Celebrities.
They hate to be recognized as Celebrities.
Hate, hate, hate.
All Celebrities dress like the man in back.
Do you know why they dress like the man in back?
So that people will know they are Celebrities.

LESSON 2.

See the Celebrity run.
Run, Celebrity, run.
He is running to see his Analyst.
All Celebrities see Analysts.
Money, money, money.
All Celebrities have problems.
All Celebrities are unhappy.
Gloom, gloom, gloom.
Why are they unhappy?
Because they are rich and famous and beautiful.
You are lucky.
You are not rich and famous and beautiful.
You are poor and unknown and ugly.
Aren't you glad you are happy?

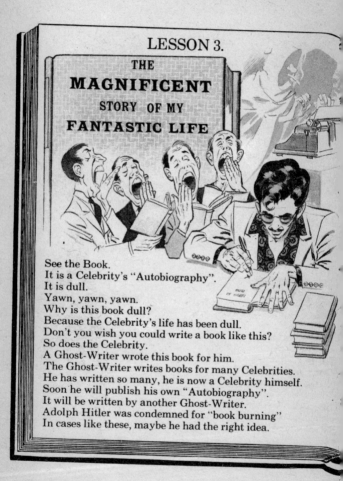

LESSON 3.

THE
MAGNIFICENT
STORY OF MY
FANTASTIC LIFE

See the Book.
It is a Celebrity's "Autobiography".
It is dull.
Yawn, yawn, yawn.
Why is this book dull?
Because the Celebrity's life has been dull.
Don't you wish you could write a book like this?
So does the Celebrity.
A Ghost-Writer wrote this book for him.
The Ghost-Writer writes books for many Celebrities.
He has written so many, he is now a Celebrity himself.
Soon he will publish his own "Autobiography".
It will be written by another Ghost-Writer.
Adolph Hitler was condemned for "book burning"
In cases like these, maybe he had the right idea.

LESSON 4.

See the "Old-Time" Celebrity.
Your Mommy and Daddy love her.
She cannot sing.
She sings.
She cannot tell stories.
She tells stories.
And she cries.
Cry, cry, cry.
Boy, does she cry.
Every performance.
This is called nostalgia.
This is also called a great "Gimmick".
She makes $30,000 a week.
And she still cries.
But it's not easy.

LESSON 5.

See the young Celebrity.
He sings.
La, la, la.
He writes songs.
Scribble, scribble, scribble.
He acts.
Emote, emote, emote.
He owns most of the Western Hemisphere.
He is a living legend.
He has been in Show Business since 3 o'clock yesterday.
He has humility.
He makes $1000 a minute.
This could only happen in America.
How much does your Teacher make?

LESSON 6.

See the lady.
She would like her son to be a Celebrity.
He is three years old.
He would like to be a Fireman.
She drags him to Casting Offices.
She drags him to Model Agencies.
He has one of two choices.
He can "make it" in Show Business.
Or she will break every bone in his body.
Crunch, crunch, crunch.
He might never make it.
But she will.
Some day she will play the title role in a Monster Movie.
She will not need make-up.

LESSON 7.

See the funny man.
His name is Marvin Finstervlep.
Soon he will get a nose job.
Bob, bob, bob.
Soon he will get a hair job.
Paste, paste, paste.
Soon he will get a name job.
Bop Crash, Bop Crash, Bop Crash.
Soon he will become a "Star"
Soon he will hate the Press.
Why will he hate the Press?
Because Reporters will annoy him.
Because they will not respect his privacy.
Because they will not let him be *himself*.

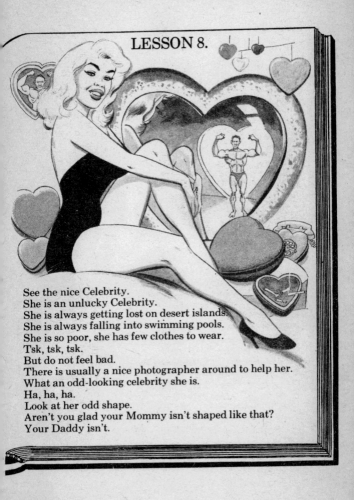

LESSON 8.

See the nice Celebrity.
She is an unlucky Celebrity.
She is always getting lost on desert islands.
She is always falling into swimming pools.
She is so poor, she has few clothes to wear.
Tsk, tsk, tsk.
But do not feel bad.
There is usually a nice photographer around to help her.
What an odd-looking celebrity she is.
Ha, ha, ha.
Look at her odd shape.
Aren't you glad your Mommy isn't shaped like that?
Your Daddy isn't.

LESSON 9.

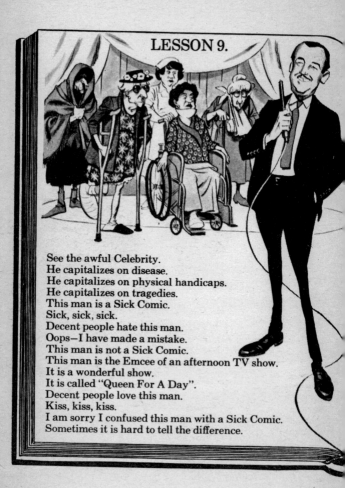

See the awful Celebrity.
He capitalizes on disease.
He capitalizes on physical handicaps.
He capitalizes on tragedies.
This man is a Sick Comic.
Sick, sick, sick.
Decent people hate this man.
Oops—I have made a mistake.
This man is not a Sick Comic.
This man is the Emcee of an afternoon TV show.
It is a wonderful show.
It is called "Queen For A Day".
Decent people love this man.
Kiss, kiss, kiss.
I am sorry I confused this man with a Sick Comic.
Sometimes it is hard to tell the difference.

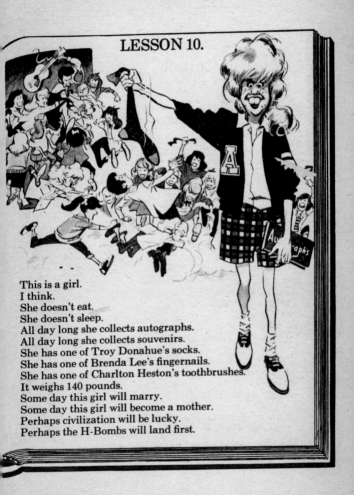

LESSON 10.

This is a girl.
I think.
She doesn't eat.
She doesn't sleep.
All day long she collects autographs.
All day long she collects souvenirs.
She has one of Troy Donahue's socks.
She has one of Brenda Lee's fingernails.
She has one of Charlton Heston's toothbrushes.
It weighs 140 pounds.
Some day this girl will marry.
Some day this girl will become a mother.
Perhaps civilization will be lucky.
Perhaps the H-Bombs will land first.

Antonio Prohias, whose anti-Communist cartoons so angered Fidel Castro that he was forced to flee Cuba, brings us another installment of that friendly rivalry between the man in black and the man in white—better known as . . .

BLUE CHIPS OFF THE OLD BLOCK DEPT.

A common practice among Big Business Organizations is to set up scholarship funds and research grants bearing their names. They do this for two important reasons: To cast a good corporate image

THE VEEBLEFETZER SCHOLARSHIP FUND

THE YERKES CARTEL FOUNDATION

THE SFORTZ CORP. STUDENT DEVELOPMENT PROGRAM

THE ZIBINDIN RESEARCH GRANT

THE CONSOLIDATED MONEY CORP. FELLOWSHIP

They do it for another reason, too. They hope that the young people who benefit by these scholarships and fellowships will eventually go to work for the corporations that sponsored them.

PRESIDENT

... and to try to make the public forget that the founders of these corporations were a bunch of money-grabbing bandits!

This type of activity is commonly known as "Philanthropic Public Service." It is also known as "Sneaky Advertising!"

However, it doesn't always work! Many people who benefit by scholarships and research funds from one corporation often go to work for competitive companies. And MAD has discovered why this happens. Big organizations are not brain-washing young men and women at an early-enough age! People in their late teens and early twenties are too independent. MAD feels that if corporations want to lure young people into joining them, they've got to go after them early in life. In fact, here's what could happen

IF CORPORATIONS

SUMMER

CAMP FORD

Hi, kids! I'm Uncle Henry! Welcome to Camp Ford. Those of you who were here in 1961 probably notice that our **new 1962 camp** is a lot **lower** and **longer**—giving you **big camp comfort** at a **small camp price.** We've also got an exciting new "Compact Mess Hall" this year, which is far superior to those in **foreign** summer camps. And as for our food, you will find that it's improved considerably. Which means your bodies will be a lot **tighter** this year!

22

RAN THEIR OWN CAMPS

TO INDOCTRINATE FUTURE EMPLOYEES OF THE FORD MOTOR COMPANY

You'll be glad to know that our "sister" camp—Camp Mercury—has been moved further up the lake, which means you'll be getting **more miles** to the **gals!**

Hey, what's that section of buildings over there covered with that **huge white sheet?**

That's the **1963** Camp Ford! I hear if we drink our milk every day, they'll lift the sheet on Labor Day, and let us take a **peek** at it!

25

CAMP BBD&O

Welcome aboard, boys! Name-wise, I'm Uncle Ozzie! We try to run a tight ship here at Camp BBD&O, and we hope you'll fall in with us, **fun-wise!** There'll be plenty of **fun-conferences**, we'll sing lots of **camp jingles**, and on Visitors' Day, you will be able to compare those **old** parents you've been using all these years with some exciting **new** parents—just in case any of you would like to make a **big change, and see.** Well, it's a hot day, so what do you say we all adjourn to the Recreation Hall for a seven-hour conference on whether or not we should go swimming, **lake-wise?**

Well, gang! It's getting a little late! We've been at this campfire conference for **five hours!** Anybody got any suggestions—**inventive-wise?**

I'm just talking off the top of my head now, Uncle Ozzie, but how does **this** sound? What do you say we **light the fire?**

What's with this Tommy and his radical ideas? What's he doing, bucking for **Vice-Counselor** or something?

CAMP M G M

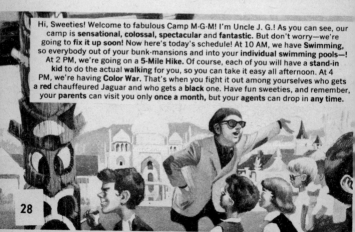

Hi, Sweeties! Welcome to fabulous Camp M-G-M! I'm Uncle J. G.! As you can see, our camp is **sensational, colossal, spectacular** and **fantastic.** But don't worry—we're going to **fix it up soon!** Now here's today's schedule! At 10 AM, we have **Swimming,** so everybody out of your bunk-mansions and into your **individual swimming pools—!** At 2 PM, we're going on a **5-Mile Hike.** Of course, each of you will have a **stand-in kid** to do the actual **walking** for you, so you can take it easy all afternoon. At 4 PM, we're having **Color War.** That's when you fight it out among yourselves who gets a **red** chauffeured Jaguar and who gets a **black** one. Have fun sweeties, and remember, your **parents** can visit you only **once a month,** but your **agents** can drop in **any time.**

TO INDOCTRINATE FUTURE SHOW BUSINESS PERSONALITIES

30

31

Don Martin, who's been handing us the same "song and dance" for years, recently came up with an idea for a new musical called "Flower Dome Song!" It happened—

IN A DOCTOR'S OFFICE

D. MARTIN

As you have seen in the previous article, a newspaper is not quite the same when "Summer Replacements" take over. And the same would go for other fields of endeavor, like when doctors, lawyers and garbage men go on vacation. Here, then, is MAD's version of what might happen . . .

IF THEY HAD SUMMER REPLACEMENTS IN EVERYDAY LIFE

IF AUTO MECHANICS WERE REPLACED BY DOCTORS

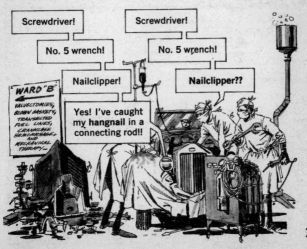

IF GARBAGE COLLECTORS

WERE REPLACED

BY MADISON AVENUE EXECUTIVES

IF CLOTHING SALESMEN WERE REPLACED BY AUTOMOBILE SALESMEN

Ah, I see you're admiring our new '62 Custom Dacron Special! You've noticed the "extras," of course, such as the **chrome zipper** and that roomy **trunk space** in the seat of the pants. Tell me, are you looking for something for the **city,** or a model for running around in the **suburbs?**

Well, I really hadn't coun—

Then may I suggest a **convertible!** That includes the suit, **and** a pair of contrasting slacks! Only a few dollars more, but a **great savings** when you consider you'll be using it for business **and** pleasure! The price is a **low $89.95,** but I can give you an **$18.50 trade-in-allowance** on that '60 **Grey-Flannel** you're wearing now. Let's see how you look in it . . .

IF BARBERS
WERE REPLACED
BY LAWYERS

44

45

IF BUS DRIVERS
WERE REPLACED
BY AIRLINE PILOTS

Good morning, ladies and gentlemen! This is your Crosstown Bus Lines Captain, Rex Hendershot, speaking! Welcome aboard Run 592. We will be departing on schedule, and will make stops at 2nd, 3rd, 4th, 5th, 6th, 7th, 8th, 9th, 10th, 11th, and Potrzebie Streets! Our cruising speed will be approximately 27 miles per hour, and we will be driving at an altitude of 245 feet above sea level, but on the ground. Our estimated time of arrival at our first stop is 8:18, or two minutes from now!

I have been informed by Bus Traffic Control that there will be a short lay-over at 4th Street due to a jammed traffic signal. The delay should not prevent passengers departing at the 6th Street transfer point from making their scheduled connection with the City Lines Bus Co.'s south-bound coach run, due to arrive at 6th Street at 8:29. However, passengers are advised to remain in their seats until the traffic signal trouble is located.

I have a report of dense traffic formations beyond 8th Street, which have clogged up the 9th Street Bus stop. This has necessitated our run being re-routed down the winding dirt road through Shady Grove Cemetery! We regret this inconvenience which will make us approximately 25 minutes late reaching our final destination. We will, however, try to make up part of this delay by reckless driving. Thank you for riding Crosstown with us, Have a pleasant run-and —Hang on!!

Today, American manufacturers spend millions of dollars in an insane drive to get you to grab their products. Giant advertising campaigns bombard you with ridiculous reasons for buying a certain brand of junk, and TV and mail promotions give you added incentives for throwing away your good money. Which is okay, if you're idiot enough to fall for them. But thank goodness the United States Government isn't subjected to this pressure — it buys from **sealed bids!** Can you imagine what it'd be like if the Government **did** buy the same way as you and I? Can't you **see** some of the TV, magazine and mail advertising campaigns Madison Ave. would come up with

IF THE U.S. GOV'T. BOUGHT LIKE THE U.S. PUBLIC BUYS

50

54

Not so! Other isotopes may be **flashier** and give a **higher radiation yield**, but they can also **foul up cyclotrons** and cause **expensive repairs.**

Say, it's **working again!** This is great! **Thanks!**

Don't thank me—thank **Westinghouse!** And remember—the makers of 16 top-loading cyclotrons all pack **Westinghouse Isotopes** in their machines!

NAME THIS NEW GENERAL DYNAMICS
I.C.B.M. ROCKET
AND
Win It!

Imagine yourself the envy of every Military Commander in the continental United States. With your own personal General Dynamics ICBM Rocket, **you're** the boss! The Pentagon listens to **you**! Comes fully operational, complete with beautiful full-color map outlining 37 suggested target areas. And it's yours **FREE!** Just give it a winning name!

HERE'S ALL YOU DO

Choose a name from list of suggestions below that you feel best describes the new General Dynamics ICBM rocket and complete this sentence in 25 words or less: "**I think the new General Dynamics I C B M Rocket should be called:**

_____

Because: _____

Suggestions:

GREEK: Icarus, Oedipus, Plato, Spyros Skouros
ROMAN: Vulcan, Pliny the Elder, Anna Magnani
GERMAN: Dancer, Prancer, Donner und Blitzen
AMERICAN: Mary Worth, Alley Oop, George Jessel

Send your entry along with the end-flap from any General Dynamics weapon crate to: Contest, Box 137, Fallout Shelter Station P. O., Wilmington, Delaware. Employees of General Dynamics and civilians not eligible. The contest closes **May 16, 1963.** Winners will be announced on special Conelrad Broadcast right after the first attack wave is completed.

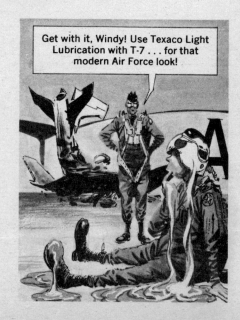

Chestnuts roasting on open fire, Jack Frost nipping at our nose
. . . Yep, that frigid season is almost upon us. So, as a special
service to all our readers, MAD presents the following feature
guaranteed to warm the heart . . . and the hands as well . . .
mainly if you put a match to it before you read it. Or better
still, use a "lighter" on—

THE LIGHTER SIDE OF
WINTER

63

65

66

68

69

Big deal! So you cleared the driveway! A lot of good **that's** going to do you if the **road** is still blocked with snow!

Listen, pal! Whaddya think I pay **taxes** for! It's the **city's** job to clear the roads — so how about comin' down here and **do that very thing** so I can get my **car** out of the driveway!!

See! All you have to do is make a little **noise**, and you get things **done**! Here comes the snow plow now! We'll be ready to go in another minute —

73

74

HAH!

Boy, there's nothing funnier then to see some pompous stuffed-shirt slip on the ice and take a prat fall!! HA-HA-HA — HO — HO-HO!!

HAH!

What's so funny?!

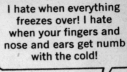

I hate Winter!!

I hate when the icy wind makes the tears run down your cheeks! I hate the blanket of snow that makes driving dangerous! I hate when it melts, and you have to slog through all that slush!

I hate when everything freezes over! I hate when your fingers and nose and ears get numb with the cold!

Oh, how I hate Winter!

Because that's when those **Yankees** come here to Florida to get away from them Northern winters! And we hate Yankees!

But we sure love them **Yankee** dollars!

77

THE CALL OF THE MILD DEPT.

Today, the trend in magazines seems to be toward specialization. Newsstands are glutted with magazines for practically everybody. "Woman's Day" is for the women . . . "Playboy" is for the playboys . . . "Good Housekeeping" is for the good housekeepers . . . "MAD" is for the birds. And then, of course, there's that rash of Men's magazines . . . for the men! "For the rugged men, that is. Magazines like "True", "Saga", "Argosy" and "Cavalier" are filled with stories of heroism, courage, blood and raw guts. But what about the gentler men—men who never kill sabre-toothed tigers with their bare hands—men who aren't heroic—who have no courage or blood or raw guts. Men like you and me! In other words, cowards! Yessiree, they really should have a magazine for our kind of people, something like

Chickens Around Town
WHAT THEY'RE DOING, AND THEN RUNNING AWAY FROM

Dellwood Bubby, who always used to complain that nasty fellows kept beating him up because he had a weak chin, grew a goatee last month. Now they're beating him up because he has a weak beard . . . Chauncy Miltown, who was told by Hans "Muscles" Schultz, his local butcher, to "Get lost!" is believed to be somewhere in the Amazon jungles . . . Finchley Weathergate was bitten by another dog again last week. This dog was named Sally Crudge . . . Wilbur Fergus and Rodney Chamois, who feed the pigeons in the park every afternoon, were attacked and severely injured by a half-crazed sparrow late Friday . . . Franklin Simon

Wilbur Fergus and Rodney Chamois
after savage attack in the park.

certainly put down a group of fellows who were making fun of him in Gallagher's Bar the other night. He got out of his chair, walked right over to them, and threw up! They won't bother him again . . . bully for you, Franklin!

* * * *

Tommy Tinker watched wrestling for the first time on his brand new television set last week. His friends will be delighted to know that he's at Johns Hopkins and recovering nicely . . . Carlton Dillingham writes that he has a new son, which is "good news"— as he puts it, because now he has someone to wear his old knickers. Unfortunately, the boy will have to wait until he's full grown, since Carlton never wore knickers as a child . . . Farley Frumpsch, who was struck by a Police Prowl Car and knocked 150 feet in the air last week, has pleaded guilty to a charge of leaving the scene of an accident.

* * * *

When Kevin Justin was mugged in the park last week, he was busy necking with Cynthia Frost. That's the third time in three months that Cynthia's mugged Kevin! You'd think he'd learn! . . .

Kevin Justin and Cynthia Frost after savage mugging in the park.

Count Renfrew Von Leardon was grossly insulted by a tough in one of the better nighteries, and the plucky Count quickly stood up to the brute and slapped him across the face with his glove. Whereupon the tough hit the Count across the face with *his* glove. Unfortunately, his fist was in it at the time! . . . Jason Flam has been riding around in a protective Police Car for the past four months. We were very excited about this news, and thought for a while that he was one of us. But he isn't. He's riding around in that car because he happens to be a cop.

83

I RECEIVED 18 MEDALS DURING WORLD WAR II

By CHUMLEY FROTH TETLEY, JR., D.F.C.

TO THOSE OF YOU who know and love me, it may seem strange and unbelievable that I personally received 18 medals during World War II, especially since I was 4-F, and rejected by every Draft Board in the State—thank goodness! But it's true, every word of it. I swear. I *did* receive them.

They kept coming in the mail all through the war. My sister, who was a WAC, was winning them.

So I would receive them from the postman, mount them on velvet in a darling frame, and keep them for her. I figured it was the least I could do for the brave girls that were giving their all on far-flung battle fields across the world to protect us 4-F's back here at home.

Which is how I earned my D.F.C. *(Dedicated Fabulous Coward)* Award. It seems my mother wrote to that wonderful organization behind my back,

The "Chicken" of the Month

"Chicken-of-the-Month"
Award

Derwood P. Freen

IN A 24-HOUR PERIOD, DERWOOD P. FREEN DISTINGUISHED HIMSELF BY THE FOLLOWING "CHICKEN" ACTS:

Entered a restaurant with a lawful seating capacity of 175 people, and after counting, discovered that he was number 176—so he promptly left.

Spotted a burning building full of screaming people, looked around, saw a large pole with a fire alarm box on it, and hid behind it for two hours until the fire was finally put out.

Confronted by a "DON'T WALK" sign which was obviously out of order and wouldn't switch to "WALK," he spent 3 hours on the corner, afraid to move, until a man came and fixed the sign.

Went across the street to a theater featuring the latest horror movie—and fainted during the color cartoon.

After the movie, came upon 3 toughs beating up a young girl. Wasting no time, he dashed into the fray, gave the girl a hard slap and ran away.

Witnessing a liquor store hold-up, he whipped out a pad and pencil, wrote down the license plate number of the getaway car, hailed a passing taxi, pursued the crooks until they passed his bookie's place, stopped, rushed in, played the number, and won $172.

Got on a bus without realizing it was filled with loud, rowdy girl scouts. 27 blocks later, got off the bus (or was pushed) with 2 black eyes, his tie in 14 knots, and 385 boxes of cookies that cost him exactly $172.

Quickly made his way up to his room, where he fearlessly donned his new "Winnie-the-Pooh" pajamas, crawled under his youth-bed, and fell asleep.

CONGRATULATIONS TO YOU DERWOOD P. FREEN, FOR WINNING THE "CHICKEN OF THE MONTH AWARD"! IT'S HERE IN OUR OFFICES, WAITING FOR YOU TO PICK IT UP...BUT WE DOUBT IF YOU HAVE THE GUTS TO COME AND GET IT!
—The Editors

THE INQUIRING CHICKEN
by Warren (Nosey) Nussbaum

QUESTION: WHY DO YOU SUBSCRIBE TO CHICKEN MAGAZINE?

TOD BLATT
Novice-Escapist

In a way, Colonel John Glenn was responsible for my introduction to Chicken Magazine. I was watching the on-the-spot news coverage of his orbital flight on television with my mother last February, and during his ride up in the elevator to the nose cone, I fainted. My mother immediately decided it was time to introduce me to Chicken and got me a gift subscription.

BILL ("HOPALONG") BOYD
Son of the Former Cowboy Star, Bill Schwartz

Ooooooh! Don't ever sneak up on a guy like that again! You scared the daylights out of me! I feel faint. Let me lean on you for a minute. I didn't see you standing there. Oh, Dear — my heart is beating like a trip-hammer. I don't think . . . I'm going to . . . make it . . . everything is . . . turning . . . black—I think I'm going to-o-o-o (THUD)

SANFORD P. GLACE
Free-Lance Fink

I subscribe to Chicken because I want to maintain my individuality in a world over-run with ruffians. I abhor cruelty, and I want everybody to know it. If more people read Chicken, there would be less violence in the world, and get that pad and pencil out of my face or I'll scratch your eyes out!

HARVEY MITTLEFUDD
Professional Coward

I subscribe to Chicken Magazine because I adore it. But it sure has given me some lumps. I used to go down to my local newsstand to buy it every month, but the neighborhood kids would wait for me and attack me, and the news dealer would hit me, and I'd come home a bloody mess. Then I got smart and subscribed. Now it's delivered to my door once a month, and the only guy that beats me up is the postman.

CHICKEN'S MONTHLY HISTORICAL QUIZ

What famous Chickens in history made these fabulous "Chicken Statements"?

"I have not yet begun to fight . . . and I don't intend to!"_____

"War is hell . . . and that's why I'm staying home!"_____

"I only regret that I have but one life to give to my country . . . but that is the case, so I'll see you around!"_____

"Don't fire until you see the whites of their eyes! That should give me enough time to get the heck out of here!"_____

"Don't give up the ship . . . sell it!"_____

"Shoot if you must this old gray head . . . it's my Grandfather's anyway!"_____

CHICKEN'S MONTHLY SPORTS CORNER

CHICKEN'S RECOMMENDED LIST OF SPORTS TO WATCH:	CHICKEN'S RECOMMENDED LIST OF SPORTS TO PLAY:
1. Bullfighting	1.
2. Karate	2.
3. Judo	3.
4. Ice Hockey	4.
5. Drag Racing	5.
6. Street Rumbling	6.
7. Park Mugging	7.
8. Jai Alai	8.

NEXT MONTH: Famous Chicken Sports Figures and Their Chicken Feats

Chicken Classified Ads

345—Job Opportunities

WORK in a tranquilizer Manufacturing Plant. $70.00 a week, and all you can swallow. Box 159, Chicken Magazine.

BOUNCERS, Immediate employment, 4 or 5 openings in a leading Tennis Ball Factory. Salary, $2.50 per hour. Box 161, Chicken Mag-

PUSHERS, Opportunity for ambitious young men to work outdoors as product testers for successful Baby Carriage Manufacturer. Write to Box 164, Chicken Magazine.

BIG GAME HUNTERS needed in Research Division of large Toy Company. Our staff has previously uncovered such big games as Scrabble, Monopoly and Backgammon. Apply Box 166.

346—Personals

MISSING, looks like typical English Sheep Dog, answers to the name of Sidney, last seen drinking water from a saucer outside restaurant corner Main and Front Sts., has leash and collar with name Sidney on it. If found, please return immediately. It's my husband! Sally Mutz. Box 2.

COMING UP IN NEXT MONTH'S

Chicken

(If Your Heart Can Stand It!)

"SOMEDAY I WILL RETURN TO THE SAVAGE AMAZON!"
By Julie Newmar's Ex-Boyfriend

"I FINALLY LEFT MY MOTHER!"
The Exciting Story Of A 45-Year-Old Bachelor's Struggle For INDEPENDENCE!

"I WAS BEATEN UP 37 TIMES IN THE THIRD GRADE!"
Sidney Finster Tells Why He Finally Gave Up Teaching

"THE MAN WHO TALKED BACK TO HIS SISTER AND LIVED!"
(Fiction)

As Americans, one of our most admirable traits is the ability we have to laugh at ourselves and make light of serious matters. Even Cape Canaveral couldn't escape the humorous onslaughts directed its way by such comic

A MAD LOOK

SPACE

Nichols and May ("But, Mother—I was sending up Vanguard!"), Bill Dana
'm gonna cry a lot!"), Charlie Manna ("I'm not goin' without my crayons!"),
. And so, in answer to many requests that we add our observations, here's

AT THE U.S.

EFFORT

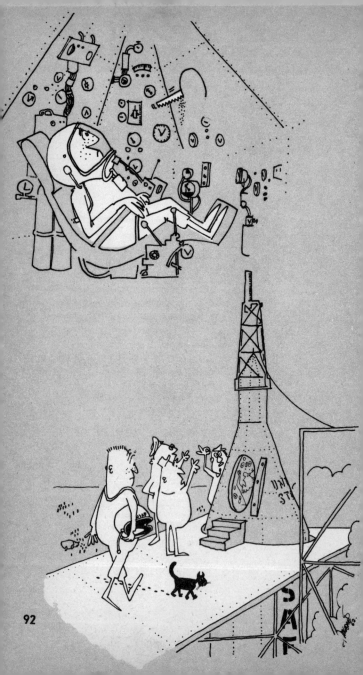

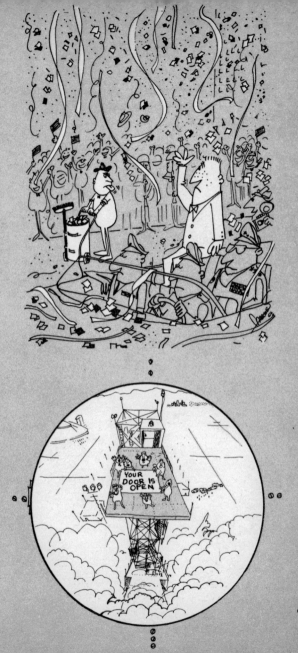

With Labor Day almost upon us, everybody is getting ready to salute the Labor Unions of America . . . Everyone that is, except the people who have to bargain with them, namely Management. MAD feels it is only fitting that Management should have the opportunity to pay its sincere respects to Organized Labor on Labor Day. And so, slightly choked up with sentiment, we now present this 1967 selection of

LABOR DAY CARDS

FROM MANAGEMENT TO LABOR

TO A
CONVICTED LABOR ORGANIZER

You've unionized upholsterers,
Mechanics and morticians,
You've unionized biologists,
Explorers and magicians;

> You've unionized from coast to coast –
> From Hollywood to Trenton;
> And now you've 10 to 20 years
> To unionize San Quentin!

TO A SUCCESSFUL STRIKING LOCAL

Your strike has lasted 40 weeks
And shows no sign of ending;
Your Union Boss is tough and firm
And shows no sign of bending;
You've made your point! We see no need
For further arbitration!
Surprise! We've used these 40 weeks
To put in automation!

TO AN UNSUCCESSFUL STRIKING LOCAL

A pity that your walkout failed,
Oh, Local 905!
We thought your Strike Fund's million bucks
Would keep your strike alive!
How could you know the money that
You filled your Union "till" with
Your ever-loyal Treasurer
Would run off to Brazil with?

TO A HIRED GANG OF PROFESSIONAL PICKETS

You rabbit-punched our president
And overturned his car;
You smashed our gates and pelted eggs;
But now you've gone too far!
No matter how you threaten us
Or yell or shout or scream—
We'll never, never let you join
Our Monday bowling team!

TO A RED-HOT
LABOR NEGOTIATOR

You've won your 20-hour week,
And that is not to mention
Your triple time for overtime,
Your pay hike, and your pension!
The contract we were forced to sign
No other firm will top;
Too bad you won't enjoy it, cause
We've had to close up shop!

TO A RAILROAD WORKER

You shovel up the coal that gives
    Our railroad trains their power;
For this your Union sees to it
    You get five bucks an hour;
So why do people say that you're
    A featherbedding weasel?
Because you know as well as we
    The whole darn railroad's *diesel*!

BUT JUST TO KEEP THINGS FAIR...

HERE ARE SOME

LABOR DAY CARDS

FROM LABOR
TO MANAGEMENT

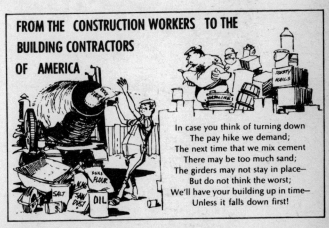

FROM THE CONSTRUCTION WORKERS TO THE
BUILDING CONTRACTORS
OF AMERICA

In case you think of turning down
The pay hike we demand;
The next time that we mix cement
There may be too much sand;
The girders may not stay in place—
But do not think the worst;
We'll have your building up in time—
Unless it falls down first!

FROM THE UNITED AUTO WORKERS
TO GENERAL MOTORS CORP.

We'll soon be sitting down with you
    to see if there's a way
To get the GM Management
    to raise our rate of pay

200,000 workers simply
    cannot be ignored;
    Cause if we are, we'll all go out
       and buy a brand new Ford!

You tried to raise the price of steel,
But much to your dismay,
You found instead you only raised
The wrath of JFK.
So now you fellows are despised
Throughout the New Frontier,
While Labor's loved—at least until
We meet again next year!

FROM THE
AMERICAN FEDERATION OF MUSICIANS
TO THE
NEW YORK PHILHARMONIC

*Other unions have their woes, but
us—we haven't any;
If we walked out, you'd only have
our music stands and Lenny;
The threat of automation fills us
with no fears and qualms;
'Cause automation just can't work
with Mozart, Bach and Brahms!*

Every year about this time the fancy slick magazines run annual "Football Roundups." We've noticed however, that these "roundups" only seem to be concerned with the big universities. What about the smaller, specialized schools? Why doesn't some magazine run a "roundup" about them? We'll tell you why! Because nobody is really interested, that's why! Which is also the general feeling about MAD. So it's only natural that we now present . . .

MAD'S FOOTBALL ROUNDUP

For Little-Known Schools and Colleges

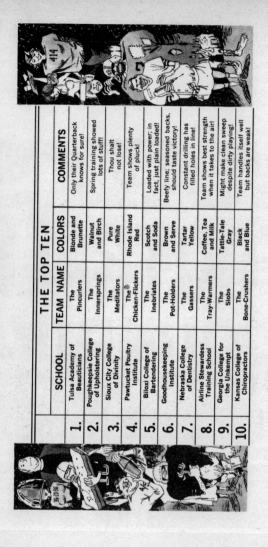

THE TOP TEN

	SCHOOL	TEAM NAME	COLORS	COMMENTS
1.	Tulsa Academy of Beauticians	The Pincurlers	Blonde and Brunette	Only their Quarterback knows for sure!
2.	Poughkeepsie College of Upholstering	The Innersprings	Walnut and Birch	Spring training showed lots of stuff!
3.	Sioux City College of Divinity	The Meditators	Pure White	Thou shalt not lose!
4.	Pawtucket Poultry Institute	The Chicken-Flickers	Rhode Island Red	Team shows plenty of pluck!
5.	Biloxi College of Bartendering	The Inebriates	Scotch and Soda	Loaded with power; in fact, just plain loaded!
6.	Goodhousekeeping Institute	The Pot-Holders	Brown and Serve	Beefy line; seasoned backs, should taste victory!
7.	Nebraska College of Dentistry	The Gassers	Tartar Yellow	Constant drilling has filled holes in line!
8.	Airline Stewardess Training School	The Tray-Warmers	Coffee, Tea and Milk	Team shows best strength when it takes to the air!
9.	Georgia College for the Unkempt	The Slobs	Tattle-Tale Gray	Might make clean sweep despite dirty playing!
10.	Kansas College of Chiropractors	The Bone-Crushers	Black and Blue	Team handles itself well but backs are weak!

HIGHLIGHTS

OF

UPCOMING

GAMES

Experts are speculating whether Akron
Academy of Acrobatics will be allowed
to run its controversial Pyramid Play.

Players from the IBM Training School will get last-minute instructions from their new IBM coach, the Mark-IV-61B.

The Western Anthropological Research Center has many strong players on its bench, ready to be sent into the game.

Players from Ohio College of Neurotics can expect emergency first aid on the field after any traumatic experience.

The fast-quipping backfield of the Ace Gagwriters Institute will continue to break up the opposition again in '67

The Florida College of Sandhogs boasts
some new offensive plays that open big
holes for its ground-gaining backfield.

SMALL COLLEGE PLAYERS
TO WATCH

Morton Meef, *Quarterback*
Montana Medical College

Carrying the ball against Iowa Medical
last year, Meef amazed spectators by a
successful removal of the bladder during a quick opener. However, the play
was diagnosed as an illegal operating
procedure, and Meef got the treatment.

Fowler Esterhazy *End*
New Mexico School of Law

This is the last season for Esterhazy, who has saved many a verdict for the "Plaintiffs" through brilliant defense. During a '66 tilt with Oregon Law, his objection to a penalty was sustained—and the Referee got 2 to 5 for perjury.

Fenwick "Sphinx" Forbusher, *Back*
Idaho Institute of Archaeology

Forbusher, who plays football for the "Tomb-Diggers", against his Mummy's wishes, won nationwide acclaim during the *1966* season when he became the first quarterback in history to call signals in "Egyptian hieroglyphics."

Horace "Pansy" Hemus, *Guard*
Brooklyn College of Botany

In *1966*, Hemus cost his team a trip to the Chlorophyll Bowl when he detoured around a rare specimen of African Violet while chasing a back from Biology Normal. However he is rated a budding lineman if he can overcome greenness.

Grover Hzcsklynski, *Center*
Arthur Murray Dance Studios

Although severely injured, Hzcsklynski still managed to sign up the entire opposition team for the October Special Six-Week Advanced Beginner's Cha-Cha Course while trapped in a pile-up in a game with Dale Carnegie Tech last year.

Felix "Orbit" Corbett, *Tackle*
Alabama College of Astrology

Corbett's horoscope is very promising
this season, which means he may get to
play. His past three seasons have been
marred by a fractured jaw, a sprained
pelvis, and the failure of Saturn to
come into conjunction with Mercury.

Myron Fink, *Fullback*
San Quentin

In last year's game with Leavenworth,
Fink found a hole in the wall, eluded
two guards and a safety man, and ran
3,279 yards before they could finally
bring him down. His wounds should heal
in time for *1967* opener with Atlanta.

Max Quibbish, *Halfback*
Texas College of Taxidermy

Quibbish set a record in '66 when he scored every time he carried the ball. This is because he reeks of formaldehyde, and nobody dares to go near him. Quibbish hopes to preserve his record for the "Skin-Stuffers" this season.

Houdini "Phhhtt" Rifkin, *End*
Michigan College of Magic

Rifkin, who failed to turn the trick for the "Rabbit-Pullers" in '66 after a mid-season suspension for turning a stadium of 25,000 spectators into a herd of gnus, seems confident for '67. Maybe he's got something up his sleeve.

HIGHLIGHTS OF UPCOMING

BAND FORMATIONS

The Texas State Crossword Puzzle Solvers Institute has two marching bands this year . . . one for horizontal formations, and one for vertical formations. The "Pencil-Sharpeners" have even bigger plans . . . they hope to field a team, too!

The Pittsfield Massachusetts College of Applied Finance and Business Administration now teaches shorthand—which means that its small marching band will finally be able to spell out the name of the school between halves this year.

The marching band of the Biloxi College of Bartendering will attempt to form its school initial, "B," again this year, but we doubt if it will succeed. Once again, the Gin and Vodka Lab Courses are scheduled for Saturday mornings.

The Indiana College of Internal Medicine won the Intricate Band Formation Award for Small Colleges in *1966* with its famous "Small Intestine Formation," which extended across the field and parking lots, and through most of the campus.

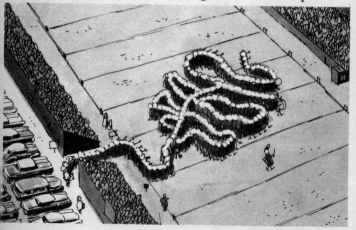

AD NAUSEUM DEPT.

Take a look through the top magazines of today and what do you see? Ads—ads—ads! That's what you see! Magazines are so full of advertisements today, there's hardly any room left for articles and stuff. And that's because magazines are almost entirely dependent on revenue from Madison Avenue to stay in business. Now . . . with publishing costs getting higher, and an increase in Postal Rates threatening, we figure it won't be long before we'll see the day . . .

WHEN ADVERTISING TAKES OVER MAGAZINES COMPLETELY

VOLUME T.C.P. *Am* NUMBER GL-70

NATIONAL GEOGRAPHIC

February, 1963

A Visit to a Columbian
Coffee Plantation   5260
JUAN VALDEZ

Among the Savage Natives
who Retired to Florida
on $300.00 a Month   5263
PHOENIX-MUTUAL

Exploring the Interior
of the U.S.A. for
Nearly-Extinct
Burma-Shave Signs   5267
N.O. LATHER

Searching Rice Fields
of the Southeast for
Vanished Vitamins   5277
UNCLE BEN

Crossing Death Valley
With the Borax
20-Mule Team   5281
THE OLD RANGER

86 Pages of Illustrations in Kodacolor

75¢ THE COPY   7 UP THE

True Story

The Truth About
MY SIN
by Fanny Lanvin

I LET ROMANCE
FADE — FADE — FADE
AWAY
(When I Breathed on
my Boyfriend's Face)

FEB 1963   25c

HE PROMISED ME EVERYTHING
(But all I got
was Arpege)

I THOUGHT
"KLOPMAN"
WAS A MAN
TO LEAN ON!

THAT RAT AT
CHASE
MANHATTAN
TOLD ME HE
WAS MY FRIEND!

THE NIGHT
MY
DEODORANT
FAILED

THE PARTING SHOT

Come closer . . .

It is a well-known fact that, in order to be successful, the TV networks believe that their own shows must be geared to what they consider to be the level of intelligence of the average viewers. And the consensus seems to be that the average TV viewer has the equivalent of a "7-year old mind"! Of course, most TV shows wouldn't suffer if this level were

INTELL

TV

GEARED TO THE "SEV

THE HUNTLEY-BRINKLEY REPORT

Hi, folks! This is Chet Huntley —

And this is David Brinkley with the up-to-the-minute exciting things happening all around the whole world! What's first, Chet? —

In Washington today, President Kennedy came out on the White House steps. **Why** did he come out on the White House steps, David?

He came out on the White House steps to **see** somebody! And who **was** that somebody? C'mon, now, Chet! You **know**! Tell us?

I'm not gonna tell you!

Please, Chet . . . ?

dropped to say a "4-year old mind"! However, there are a
ew intellectual programs around which are aimed consider-
bly higher . . . like at a "15-year old mind"! But these shows
an't last! They'll have to change their formats or go off the
air. And so, seeing as how this change is inevitable, let's
ake a MAD look at . . .

ECTUAL
SHOWS
EN-YEAR-OLD MIND"

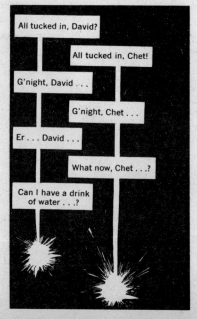

130

OPEN END

Good evening — and welcome to another edition of "Open End." Our guests tonight are all distinguished journalists, and our topic is "The Berlin Crisis." Gentlemen, shall we begin our discussion . . .?

I . . . I . . . I . . . I think 'cause like there **is no crisis** and I mean like 'cause everybody knows nuthin' about nuthin' and they're all — they're all makin' mountains outta mole hills and like that and . . . so there!

Boy-oh-boy! Are you a dummy! Oh, boy-oh-boy-oh, boy! **No crisis?** Oh, boy!

Oh yeah! Well, that's what I said and that's what I mean and there **is no crisis,** so there! And two for flinching!!—

So what! Boy, are you a **dummy!** And — and I suppose the cold war is nuthin' but a fig — a fig — a figment of — and 'cause boy, are you a **big dummy!**

THE TWENTIETH CENTURY

The PRUDENTIAL INSURANCE COMPANY of AMERICA presents: "The Twentieth Century!"

And here is your host . . . Walter Cronkite!

Tonight, on "The Twentieth Century" — "D-Day" — the invasion of Europe during World War II — actual scenes of the mightiest battle of the war — the battle that opened the door and paved the way to the liberation of France, Belgium, The Nether — The Nether — Holland, and all them other countries there!

The time, June 6th, 1944 — the greatest naval armada in history waits off the coast of Normandy as dawn breaks! Now hold your ears! 'Cause all them big cruisers and battleships are gonna start shootin' off their cannons . . . **KA — BOOOOOOOM!!!**

Here comes the planes! Boy are they ever gonna blast that beach! Wowee— lookit them bombs drop— **TWEE-E-E-E — BAROOMM! CHU-BOOM! KA-ROOM!!** Now they're strafing any dirty Nazi who may be still hanging around! **RAT-TAT-TAT-TAT-TAT—**

Here come the landing barges! —
**E-e-e-a-a-r-r-r- BOOOOOMM!
RAT-TAT-TAT! WHIRP!-WHIRP-WHIRP!**
Okay, boys! Hit that beach!
**BLAM! Chugga-chugga-chugga!
PTSHOOMM! Budd-budda-budda!
CRACK! Twaing! Tweeng! Dwaayng!
DJOOP! DJOOP!** Dig in! Dig in!
**Shhhh-oooooommm! Twee-e-e-e-e-e-
TSHAGOOOMMB!
RAT-A-TAT-TAT! BLAM! BLAM!**

Next week on "The Twentieth Century" — the
launching of our Ranger Moon Probe! You'll
visit the blockhouse, see the count-down,
track the missile . . . and you'll hear me go
**"PS-S-S—! SHW-O-O-O-O-SH!
BEEP-BEEP-BEEP-BLOINK dzzzt!** Yuh goofed it!
NYAH-NYAH, YUH GOOFED IT!"
That's next week on "The Twentieth Century!"
Now, for Prudential — this is Walter Cronkite!
Nightie-night!

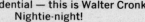

How do you do. My name is Lawrence Spivak. I am a moderator. I am the moderator on "Meet The Press." I moderate. That's what a moderator does. Don't you wish **you** were a moderator? Don't you wish **you** were the moderator on "Meet The Press?" **I do!** Then I could **stay home** on a nice Sunday afternoon like this!

See today's guest. His name is Sen. Barry Goldwater. He is our guest because we invited him. We have invited him to "Meet The Press!" See the four members of the Press. See how anxious they are to meet the Senator. See how anxious they are to ask him questions. See how anxious they are to make a fool of him. Oh! Oh! Here is the first question . . .

I have a question. I have a very tough question to ask. I have a very tough question to ask the Senator — except that from talking like this, I have **forgotten** the question. Oh! Oh! Now I remember! What is a **Conservative Republican?** How does he differ from a **Liberal Republican?** That is my question!

See the Senator! See how he squirms in his chair! Why does he squirm in his chair! He squirms because he is in the "Hot Seat." The "Hot Seat" is a seat that is hot. Why is the seat hot? The seat is hot because there is a short circuit in the Senator's microphone, and he is being slightly **electrocuted!** Ha! Ha! See him squirm! Funny Senator! Funny, funny Senator!

I am a Conservative Republican! I am called a Conservative because I want to **conserve**. I want to conserve **money**. I want to conserve **your** money. I want to take it out of **your** Piggy Bank and conserve it in **my** Piggy Bank. That is known as Free Enterprise. I like Free Enterprise. Don't you like Free Enterprise? Why don't you like Free Enterprise? Because you'd rather conserve your **own** money? Oh! You are a Liberal!!

See the Senator! See the Senator getting up! See the Senator leaving the TV studio! Why are you leaving the studio Senator? Didn't you understand the **question?**

Oh, yes! I understood the question! That is not why I am leaving! I am leaving because I didn't understand my **answer!**

Riding the wave of popularity he recently achieved as author of a paperback book, MAD'S maddest artist, Don Martin—who often goes off the deep end—now relates his abridged version of a tall tale ... mainly the time he went

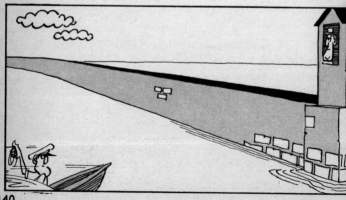

SKIING

DRAW BRIDGE

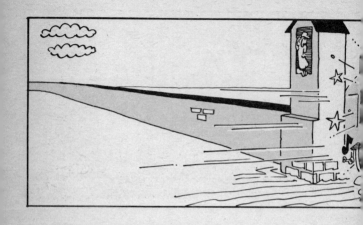

SWEET RIDE OF YOUTH DEPT.

The results of the recent physical fitness tests proved that the youth of America is in pretty bad shape. We could've proved that without those tests since we know the kind of junk it reads, like this magazine f'rinstance. Anyway, it was shown that teen-agers in this country trailed those of other nations in almost every aspect of physical fitness. The results

MODERN

SPO

were termed "shocking." But actually there's no reason to be shocked. All one has to do is study just what teen-agers do to account for these results. Today's youth has cast aside muscle-building sports like Baseball, Football, Punchball and Horseshoe Pitching, and has replaced them with "softer" activities like the following

TEENAGE

RTS

HAIR SETTING

In the past, in order to spend hours in front of a mirror setting hair, you had to be either a girl, or a toupee maker, or else you were a "sissy," and run off the block. Today, it's a big thing for fellows to take an interest in hairdos, working up odd, unusual styles like the Sal Mineo "curl," the Fabian "wave," the Jack Kennedy "bush" and the Van Cliburn "ecch." One N.Y. teenager walks around in curlers. It doesn't impress girls— but it **does** keep him out of the army!

CAR LEANING

A shade lazier than just "Standing On The Corner," this has become a leading outdoor activity. Leaning on cars four weekday evenings and all day Saturday seems to be average. The usual number is three boys per car. Once, nine boys leaned on a large car as a gag, but the owner of the Hearse chased them away. Amusing results are obtained when six-footers lean on Volkswagens. Even more amusing results are obtained when cars drive off without a warning to leaners.

PARTY CRASHING

This is a perennial favorite, indulged in by teenagers who can't get dates or who don't feel like "car leaning" on a particular evening. As a precautionary measure, it is best to know in advance just **what** kind of party you're crashing. Recently, some party crashers ran into a streak of bad luck when they crashed in succession: A "Surprise Party" for Rocky Graziano, a Philadelphia Eagles victory supper, and a P.T.A. tea-dance.

BALCONY CAVORTING

"Movie Balcony Necking," although still with us, has been slowly overtaken by good-natured boisterous carryings-on whenever teenagers without dates gather up there. Most popular of these activities are: laughing at the wrong parts of the movie, hysterically cheering the cartoon, stamping and whistling when there are technical difficulties with the film, and of course that all-time favorite: running out side exits, leaving them open for light to stream in.

SHOULDER PUNCHING

One of the more "active sports," this activity involes some physical effort. Shoulder punching is the new way to say "Hello." It has replaced the hand shake, the back slap and the light tap across the chin. When a friend approaches, the teenager says, "Howya doin', Phil?," and punches him in the shoulder. Many boys have adopted this method as the "sheik" way of saying goodnight to a blind date. Instead of kissing her, they punch her on the shoulder. Good for plenty laughs.

STRAW WRAPPER BLOWING

This activity has steadily increased in popularity over the years until now it is considered the "thing to do" when in restaurants. Participation in it is at its greatest, however, in school lunchrooms throughout the nation. Involves tearing off end of straw wrapper, then blowing it in somone's face—a nearby girl, a waitress, or a stranger at the next table. Usually results in hysterical laughter, and a punch in the mouth.

WINDOW SHOUTING

Six or eight guys pile in a car and go cruising down the main street. The one sitting in the front on the right (who is usually the best "make-out") becomes the "Window Man." He leans out as they pass females, and shouts clever, daring pick-up phrases like "Say, aren't you Doc Finster's daughter?," "Wanna lift?," "Hubba-hubba!" and "Man, I go ape over freckles!" Then they go and shout these same clever phrases at women **under** 40!

KNUCKLE CRACKING

This sport regained prominence several years back when everyone was doing Ed Sullivan imitations. Teenagers find it a simple way to kill five or six hours on a Saturday night when there is nothing else to do. It is also helpful during trying, anxious moments like taking an exam, or proposing marriage, or even writing this article. When a youngster is discovered doing knuckle cracking by his parent, it usually results in wrist slapping (see: "Modern Adult Sports").

FREELOADING

A sport mastered by many teenagers, the idea being to secure as many free meals and services as long as possible, without anyone getting wise. Freeloading at a date's home is most common. If folks begin supper without inviting teenager, he drops hints that he's hungry—like offering to pay for one of their sandwiches or saying "Boy, that looks good! Do you mind if I dig in?", pointing to the dog's dish. Prepares teenagers for marriage, when freeloading is necessary.

TWIST WATCHING

While 1% of teenagers actually dance the "Twist," 99% watch. Watching TV Dance Parties has become the teenager's number one sport. Not only the "Twist," but other dances like the "Fly," "Slop," "Stroll," "Mashed Potatoes," and "Two Fat Girls Dancing Together" are pretty exciting to watch. It may even lead to foot tapping on the part of the viewer. Heavy foot tapping combined with dial twisting can bring on teenage fatigue.

Through the magic of the motion picture camera (with the aid of a little dramatic coaching, a little careful lighting, and a whole lot of make-up), we've come to know many famous Hollywood celebrities. But actually, all we've really come to know is the image they project from the silver screens in our neighborhood theatres. What about the image they project in real life? Like f'rinstance from the silver screens in their own homes? Here is MAD'S idea of what we'd see if we were treated to some private showings of . . .

CELEBRITIES'

HOME

MOVIES

I am **ALFRED HITCHCOCK!** The delightful scenes you are about to see are from my home movies . . .

This is my daughter and son-in-law during our recent visit to Paris . . .

This is my daughter and son-in-law when we visited San Francisco . . .

Here we are while visiting Egypt . . .

This scene was shot by a friend in a plane while we were visiting N.Y.C.

Every so often, I try to appear for a fleeting moment in my home movies . . .

Hi! I'm **MICKEY ROONEY** — with a scene from my home movies . . .

Here I am, as usual, waving goodbye—

Seems like I'm always waving goodbye—

I'm waving goodbye to my wife—who is taking the picture . . . Bye-bye, honey!

I'm waving goodbye to my wife because she's leaving for Reno to divorce me!

Bye-Bye, Honey! Y'know, I can never remember which of my five wives took which scene where I'm waving bye-bye!

FOR SALE
CASH NEEDED
FOR
ALIMONY
PAYMENTS

Hi! I'm **LLOYD BRIDGES** — and here are some of my home movies! This was taken of me at the seashore!

RICHARD CHAMBERLAIN
—better known as Dr. Kildare—with a
home movie of me on Thanksgiving Day!

We read a lot about "Family Living" and "Togetherness" in the "*Women's Magazines*" these days. (We read a lot about *another* kind of living in the "*Men's Magazines*" these days, but that's a different article, and we don't feel like getting arrested!) Anyway, while the Women's Magazines extol the delights of domesticity, they rarely mention the irritations that can sometimes make homelife miserable! And, so, as a Public Service, we herewith direct the attentions of the nation's gadget manufacturers to these visionary devices, all designed to make for more harmonious households. In other words, we now present

MAD'S MODERN AIDS TO HAPPIER LIVING

IRRITATION: *Garage Gashing*

If Mom's penchant for hitting the garage with the family car piles up repairs for wrinkled fenders that drive Dad close to strangling his spouse . . .

. . . We recommend installing . .

THE PLAYTEX LIVING GARAGE

IRRITATION: *Video Vexation*

In every family, there's one person who loves a TV program that no one else can stand. If so . . .

. . . The non-conforming viewer can indulge his stubborn whim to his heart's content by installing to the front of the television set this light-proof, sound-proof . . .

PRIVATE TV TUNNEL

IRRITATION: *Fink Paper Boy*

If your paper boy always takes deadly
aim at a puddle whenever he can . . .

. . . You can insure yourself a dry
paper every time by using this . . .

FAKE PLASTIC RAIN PUDDLE

IRRITATION: *Fried Father*

If the man of the house comes home in disgraceful shape when he has a wild night out with the boys . . .

. . . This device will make him fit to face the family again. It's called . . .

DADDY'S DRUNK TANK

IRRITATION: *Icky Sticky Goo*

If feeding the baby is a horribly messy
and emotionally trying time for Mom . . .

. . . This simple device will hold both
tempers and cleaning bills down. It's

THE MOTHER & BABY FEEDING PONCHO

IRRITATION: *Tobacco Tension*

After a long, hard day, Dad is certainly entitled to relax
with a good cigar. If, however, his family can't stomach it . . .

. . . He could have his smoke and still
keep his dependents happy by using . . .

THE STOGIE SPACE HELMET

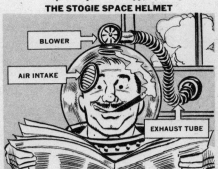

IRRITATION: *Morning Animosity*

If Mom and Dad both look awful in
the morning, and are getting sick
of the sight of one another . . .

. . . They can show each other their sunniest smiles each morning with . . .

BREAKFAST TABLE PHOTO PLACARDS

IRRITATION: *Plethora of Playthings*

If Mom can't stand it when children's
toys are constantly underfoot . . .

. . . Equip the playroom with all-metal toys, and this ingenious high-powered
gadget that snatches up any item not actually clenched in a little fist . . .

THE ELECTRO-MAGNETIC TOY CADDY

According to the experts, young people like to read MAD because it pokes fun at the "adult" world. This doesn't exactly explain why adults like to read MAD, but who are we to argue with the experts. Anyway, for those adults, here's an article that pokes fun at the "kid" world — and we'll see if young people can "take" a joke as well as "make" one . . . as MAD looks at . . .

LIGHTER

TEEN

THE

SIDE OF

AGERS

Speaking about school . . . did you notice that dreamy Carl Klutz in History class today?

Yes, and that keen Dick Drab who sits next to him! And that he-man, Bob Schmaltz! And—

CREATIVE BOY CHASING

Do you realize that all we ever talk about is **boys**? Let's talk about something **else** for a change!

You're right! Let's talk about . . . er—uh— **Sports Cars!**

Speaking about Sports Cars . . . did you notice that cute Roger Kaputnik in his new Thunderbird?

Yes, and that good-looking Kevin Finster sitting next to him, and that he-man Tony Glopp in the back?

And that groovy group: Kirk Comb, Gregory Sideburns, Rick Dribble and Chet Bagel—who were standing next to the car?

See? I **told** you! Isn't talking about **Sports Cars** much more **interesting** than talking about **boys**?!

179

Get a load of that Gwendolyn and Marsha and Gertrude!

Boy, what **dogs**!

Yeah! They're charter members of the Girls Kennel Club!

Lookit that Gwendolyn—with her ugly buck teeth!

And that Marsha—with a nose like Shnozzle Durante!

And that fat lump of blubber—Gertrude!

WE SELL BLADELESS KNIVES WITHOUT HANDLES

Girls **that homely** should be lined up against a wall and **shot**!

I'll say!

Yeah!

186

187

I'll never get rid of them!

I've tried every medication! None of them help!

My doctor says I've got to stay away from sweets!

WE SELL CONTACT LENSES WITH FRAMES

sob sob sob

Shirley, darling! What's wrong?

Oh, Mother! I'm so miserable! I'm the **only** girl in the whole crowd who **hasn't got pimples!** sob

189

IN A SICILIAN RESTAURANT